The General Care and Maintenance of
Savannah Monitors
and
Other Popular Monitor Species

by
Michael Balsai

Table of Contents

Introduction 1

General Information 2

The Savannah Monitor: General Information 3

Selecting a Savannah Monitor 11

Housing and General Maintenance 14

Feeding 21

Grooming 25

Developing a "Pet/Owner" Relationship 28

Disorders and Diseases 31

Breeding 38

Notes On Other Monitor Species 43

Source Materials 53

Introduction

Monitor lizards are among the largest, most active, and most intelligent of all the living species of squamate reptiles (i.e., lizards and snakes). Unfortunately, 4 out of the 37 or so species of monitors are already classified by CITES (Convention on International Trade in Endangered Species of Wild Fauna and Flora) under Appendix I as endangered, and all the rest are listed under Appendix II. This means that they are threatened and could become vulnerable if the trade in these species is not regulated. Because of their large size, monitor lizards (particularly savannah monitors, Nile monitors, and Asian water monitors) figure prominently in the reptile leather trade. As a side business, certain parts of their bodies are utilized to produce "exotic" souvenirs (such as their feet for key-rings). Several monitor species also serve as a source of food in their countries of origin. Finally, monitor lizards are fairly popular in the pet trade because of their large size, their often exquisite color patterns, their intelligence, the relative ease of their maintenance, and possibly, their alleged "dinosaur-like" and impressive appearance.

The ruthless exploitation of many of the species of monitors is causing their populations to decline. The availability of certain species, especially the Asian ones, has become dramatically reduced. In fact, the general rarity of monitors and pythons in certain parts of Asia has been implicated for the dramatic rise of rodent pest problems in these areas! The two sub-Saharan African species, however, are still available in reasonable numbers, but changing awareness towards the wildlife of Africa, coupled with the political instability in many of their countries, may change this in the future. Captive breeding of monitor lizards is not common, due to its relative difficulty, so virtually all specimens sold in the pet trade are wild-collected/imported animals (there are occasional exceptions).

Probably, the most popular and readily obtainable species of monitor is the savannah monitor (*Varanus exanthematicus*), an African species. Their popularity stems from the fact that they usually tame very well and do not reach the huge sizes of some other species. They are also, seemingly, the least expensive of all the monitors currently sold in the trade. A few other species can presently be had as well, and of these, the Nile monitor (*Varanus niloticus*) and the mangrove monitor (*Varanus indicus*) appear most commonly and also relatively inexpensively. This book was written to provide essential information on the responsible husbandry of the savannah monitor and other monitor species regularly offered in the pet trade.

The author would like to acknowledge the assistance of Philippe de Vosjoli and especially note his two books: *The General Care and Maintenance of the Green Iguana* and *The General Care and Maintenance of Burmese Pythons including notes on Other Large Pythons*, for the organization and inspiration of this book. The author also thanks Greg Naclerio, Pete Strimple and especially, Mark Bayless for suggesting and/or supplying references.

General Information

Monitors are moderate to large sized lizards belonging to a single genus *Varanus* within the family *Varanidae*. Their closest living relatives are the helodermids (Gila monsters and Mexican beaded lizards) and an extremely rare, obscure animal called the Bornean earless lizard, *Lanthanotus borneensis*. Many herpetologists also believe that monitors and their kin may be the closest lizard relatives of snakes. Some obvious characteristics of monitors are their long, slender, deeply forked tongues, sharp (usually) fang-like, compressed teeth, their (usually) long necks with fairly short bodies, large eyes with round pupils, the moderately large, deeply inset openings of their ears, long heads with pointed snouts, five-toed feet with large, sharp, recurved claws, long, muscular, non-breakable tails, and the total absence of femoral pores and anal glands.

DISTRIBUTION AND SIZE

There are approximately 37 living species of monitors, and of these, two thirds are natives of Australia. The rest range through Africa, tropical Asia, the Middle East, and certain Pacific Islands. While a couple of Australian species only reach a total length of 10 to 12 inches, most species average total lengths of 3 or more feet, making them the largest of all the living lizards. Monitors are completely predatory with the exception of one species from the Philippines called Gray's monitor (*Varanus olivaceus*, formerly *V. grayi*) which is omnivorous and is known to devour fruits and seeds, along with small vertebrates, eggs, snails, and insects (Auffenberg, 1988). The tree monitor (*Varanus prasinus*) may also eat fruit as captives (Sprackland, 1991b).

Adult white-throated monitor (*Varanus exanthematicus albigularis*). It has recently been proposed that this subspecies of the savannah monitor be given species status as *Varanus albigularis*. Photo by Glen Carlzen.

The Savannah Monitor: General Information

WHAT'S IN A NAME?

Varanus is a late Latin term derived from the Arabic *Waran* which literally means monitor lizard. The name "monitor" is believed to arise from an ancient superstitious belief that these lizards would give a warning when crocodiles were nearby (perhaps because Nile monitors are often seen about crocodile nests, feeding on the eggs). The species epithet *exanthematicus* is derived from the Greek word *exanthema* which means eruption and refers to any eruptions or pimples caused by disease. When applied to savannah monitors, it apparently refers to the rather large pimple-like scales on the back of the neck.

SUBSPECIES AND DISTRIBUTION

There are four subspecies of the savannah monitor, an African species, that are generally recognized as valid. These were originally categorized by Mertens in 1942. They are *Varanus exanthematicus exanthematicus*, *V. e. microstictus*, *V. e. angolensis*, and *V. e. albigularis*. All these subspecies are distinguished by variations in the number of scales around the body, and variations in the number of ventral scale rows extending from the gular (throat) fold to the upper thighs. The subspecies most commonly seen in pet stores is *Varanus e. exanthematicus*. This subspecies averages about 3 feet (1 meter) in total length and tends to be grayish-tan in color with fairly large light-gray (sometimes light blue) spots with dark brown borders along the back and sides. It ranges from Senegal in the west, to Eritrea in the east, to the Adrar mountains and the Sahara in the north, and to the rain forests of the southwest.

Varanus e. microstictus is also about 1 meter (3 feet) in total length, but the overall body color is darker than *V. e. exanthematicus*. It has large, very light colored, almost squarish spots with dark borders. It ranges throughout most of eastern Africa, from Ethiopia and Somalia in the north, then south to Kenya.

V. e. albigularis, the so-called Cape monitor, has a somewhat shorter, blunter snout than either of the above two subspecies and has been suggested by some to be a different species (*V. albigularis*). The top of the head and neck are dark brown and the back is a dark gray-brown. Cape monitors are also patterned with 5-6 rows of pale yellow dark bordered blotchy spots. The limbs are spotted with pale yellow and the tail has an alternating pattern of dark-brown and off-white bands. The belly is dirty yellow with some spotting and can be more colorful than the pale whitish or tannish bellies of the above two types. The Cape monitor is among the most attractive of all the subspecies, but is rumored to have a somewhat nastier temperament than the others. It ranges from Zimbabwe and Botswana in the north, to Namibia in the west, and east from Mozambique to south into South Africa. *V. e. angolensis* shows some minor scale variation with respect to *V. e. albigularis*, but is otherwise similar. It ranges from Angola, north into Zaire. Both of these latter two forms attain total lengths from about 3.9 feet (1.1 m) to a bit over 4.3 feet (1.3 m) (although there are reports of *V. e. albigularis* reaching lengths of 6.6 feet (2 m).

In 1964, it was proposed that another subspecies may exist called *V. e. ionidesi* which is presumed to hail mostly from Tanzania. It is believed by others to be a form of *V.e. microstictus*. *V. e. ionidesi* is distinguished mostly in terms of a presumed distinctive immature coloration, which resembles that of juvenile *V. e. albigularis* (and may argue against the former being a separate subspecies).

It is of interest to note the origin of the vast majority of savannah monitors sold in the pet trade. Ghana, Kenya, Togo, and Tanzania are the major sources, with supposedly 90% coming from Togo alone. Ghana is responsible for about 9% and virtually all the rest come from Kenya and Tanzania (Bayless, 1991; Luxmoore et al, 1988).

SEXING, GROWTH, AND LONGEVITY

Sexing savannah monitors (or any monitor) is a tricky business. Like all lizards (and all squamates for that matter), male monitors have paired hemipenes, but any examination of external characteristics will be inconclusive. Savannah monitors (as do at least a few other monitor species) also seem to have an unusual sex chromosome heteromorphism, but genetic testing is not an option for most herpetoculturists. Inducing the eversion of the hemipenes in full grown monitor lizards is a difficult procedure at best, albeit males will often briefly evert these organs after defecation. Herpetoculturists have sometimes resorted to probing and manually everting the hemipenes in juveniles with varying degrees of success or reliability.

Recently, a method has been established that will cause the eversion of hemipenes following the injection of sterile saline (either physiological saline or lactated Ringer's solution) into the tail (see Stewart, 1989). Position the needle at about where the tip of a hemipenis would be farthest from the cloaca, on the underside of the tail. Insert the needle intramuscularly and inject the saline. The volume required varies with the size of the lizard. The injected fluid "surrounds" the hemipenes and simulates vascular pressure on the organs causing them to evert (20 ml was reported to cause eversion in gila monsters, which are roughly about the size of most captive savannah monitors). Moistened or lubricated fingers can gently reinsert the organs. The lizard should be placed on a clean non-absorbent surface (such as an empty aquarium) for a few hours to prevent damage to a hemipenis, should it re-evert. This technique is ineffective on very large monitors, probably because their hemipenis retractor muscles are strong enough to overpower the injection pressure. Anesthesia may assist the relaxation of these muscles in such cases.

The San Diego Zoo attempted to determine the sex of two Komodo monitors by testing their blood for testosterone (male hormone) levels. John Weigel (1988) suggested subjecting monitor lizards to radiographic (X-ray) analysis for sex determination, presumably because at least some of the varanid species have small bones in the hemipenis (Shea and Reddacliff,1986).

BREEDING
Monitors, including savannah monitors, are difficult to breed as captives, though it has been done on various occasions, with several species (including *V. e. albigularis*), by a few zoos and individuals. Certainly, no species is regularly bred; at least that is the impression derived from scanning the literature. Data on hatchlings and egg sizes are difficult to find. However, "newborn" Cape monitors (NOTE: most of the data that follows is based on that collected for Cape monitors, except where noted) were recorded at lengths of 7.9-8.5 in. (20-21.7 cm) in length (one assumes this is total length, albeit the source did not specify) and weighed 0.83-1.01 ounces (23.6-28.6 grams). An adult can measure over 3.28 feet (1 m) and weigh 11+ pounds (5 kg). A West African hatchling was reported to be 5.5 in. (14 cm) in total length (no weight was given). Egg clutch sizes are logged in at 8 to as high as 50 eggs and various accounts of egg sizes give a range of 2.1 in. to 2.4 in. by 1.3 in. to 1.5 in. (5.3 cm to 6.1 cm by 3.4 cm to 3.9 cm).

The incubation periods for eggs laid by captives vary between 120 to about 170 days (at a temperature of between 32°C to 33°C), while in the wild it may take as long as 12 months! Mating is recorded to occur in August to mid-October with eggs laid in November through January. Females may dig a shallow nest for the eggs or deposit them in termite nests.

GROWTH
This author has observed that very young savannah monitors can increase their weight as much as 5 to 10 fold in the first year, and increase their lengths at least 2-2.5 fold during that time! This is assuming they are kept under optimal captive conditions and depends on their feeding regimen. Unfortunately, so far, no published data (to the best of this author's knowledge) is available for the rates of growth in any monitor species, nor is there any such data which indicates at what age growth tapers off. Longevity of most individuals, if not all species can be significant. Records kept on savannah monitors have shown them to reach ages of 11+ years. Other species of monitors have been recorded at ages of 15 or more years, with some of these individuals recorded as being still alive when the age was noted.

A captive-raised one year old savannah monitor (*Varanus e. exanthematicus*) on top of a three year old captive-raised male. Photo by Chris Estep.

A tame captive-raised savannah monitor checking out the face of a friend. "Dog tame" is an expression sometimes used to describe unusually tame monitors such as this one. Photo by Chris Estep.

WHAT TO CONSIDER BEFORE GETTING A SAVANNAH MONITOR

Of the few species of monitors readily available in the pet trade, savannah monitors are among the least expensive and easiest to obtain. They do not achieve the "gigantic" size (for lizards) that certain other species can reach and they (particularly *V. e. exanthematicus*) generally have reliably docile dispositions. Like most reptiles, they are not noisy and do not demand the amount of attention that cats, dogs or birds require, nor do they cause the allergy problems that mammals and birds do. Savannah monitors feed upon whole animal foods, such as rodents, and need a fairly large amount of space. Remember, that the "cute" little lizard in the pet store that is only 7-8 inches (18 or 20 cm) long will grow very fast if kept properly and will eventually require a large enclosure. If the animal is flighty or aggressive it can be a bit of a challenge to handle. Also, one should be aware that little savannah monitor lizards will grow to be large carnivorous lizards with sharp claws on powerful limbs and with sharp teeth in very strong jaws. They sometimes also use their tails as weapons. Bites from these lizards can be severe, can become infected easily, and sometimes may require stitches! So handle them with care and respect.

If the above has not deterred you, then you must know that savannah monitors are intelligent (for lizards), often beautifully colored, and fascinating as vivarium subjects. These monitors are well known for usually becoming tame in captivity, and some become almost "dog-tame." They respond to their owners to some degree and quickly learn certain routines like feeding time and cage cleaning time. The challenge of breeding these lizards should become of increasing interest to herpetoculturists, particularly when the long-term results would be a decreased demand for wild-caught specimens.

RESPONSIBLE SAVANNAH MONITOR OWNERSHIP

Savannah monitor lizards are intelligent reptiles which, in captivity, have a lot of time on their hands. In no time at all, the average healthy, inquisitive monitor will be searching for a way to expand its horizons. In other words, monitors are very good at escaping improperly secured enclosures. They also have no respect whatsoever for any household objects and some love to climb. Should your pet escape, it can wreak havoc within a matter of minutes and potentially cause damage to personal property. It might even injure itself. These lizards are also good at getting into vents and between walls or into moderately large openings of any sort. If a large savannah monitor lizard escapes to the outside during the warmer weather, its perambulations and adventures can gain you (and, perhaps, indirectly, all herpetoculturists) a significant amount of notoriety. Should your pet encounter a large dog it can almost certainly be injured or more likely killed. If it escapes outside in colder weather, you will definitely have a valuable and wonderful animal die from negligence.

When keeping monitor lizards, or any other large reptile for that matter, this author advocates some of the views of the board of The American Federation of Herpetoculturists. This non-profit organization is an advocate for the interests of serious herpetoculturists while also having sensitivity for the interests of the welfare of the general public and the amphibians and reptiles themselves. The AFH emphasizes responsible herpetoculture as the foundation of its position on keeping amphibians and reptiles as captives. Recently, the AFH outlined some views which, though targeted particularly at the ownership of snakes, especially large constrictors, have some applicability to the keeping of other reptiles as well. These considerations can be summarized as follows:

1. The general public has a right not to be unexpectedly exposed to reptiles and, in consideration of the potential for irresponsible behavior among some owners, the AFH recommends that reptiles not be displayed openly in public unless they are part of an appropriate forum for such a display (i.e., herpetological shows, pet stores, educational displays, or presentations or displays where the public is warned that reptiles may be openly displayed).

2. The AFH recommends that all reptiles be transported in a way that excludes their escape. Some moderately large lizards can be placed in large strong "snake" bags (free of holes or tears) which can be placed inside a container with holes for proper ventilation. This container should be sealed until it needs to be opened. Larger specimens need to be housed in some type of escape-proof travel cage or locking container. The cages sold to ship dogs or cats via the airlines are very useful for this purpose (though not necessarily for air travel), as long as they can be secured against accidental opening. Airlines should be consulted when shipping large reptiles by air.

3. When keeping reptiles, the caging requirements should ensure that these animals are also restricted to the confines of the owner's property. The cage should be such that the animal cannot escape from its confines. The door or cage access should be secured with locks. Ideally, cages with large monitors should be kept within a large locked room that will further ensure that the reptile cannot escape from within it. The door to the room should be kept locked and shut when not occupied by the owner. Such responsible herpetological practices ensure the safety of the reptiles, family members, and members of the general public. All herpetoculturists will benefit from these responsible practices.

4. When any large reptile is handled, it is recommended that another person be present in case of some unexpected mishap. While the possibility of a serious problem is remote, it is important to remember that large monitors can inflict serious bites and lacerations with their claws. So, safety should always be a primary consideration. Except with very tame specimens, long heavy gauntlet-like gloves will be required for handling large monitors.

5. The AFH does not recommend the ownership of snakes over seven feet by minors without parental consent and the willingness of the parents to assume responsibility to assure responsible husbandry, handling, maintenance etc. This author proposes that this should also apply to large monitor lizards, particularly any specimen over about two feet, as specimens this large are quite capable of giving severe bites and inflicting lacerations with their claws.

6. Remember, like any other pet owner, the herpetoculturist is liable for damages and medical costs inflicted by their charges upon another's person and/or property! The AFH is drafting an official statement on keeping large reptiles, such as monitor lizards, by private individuals, as well as a legislative package to assist herpetocultural societies contend with legal issues relating to these matters.

For information, write to: The American Federation of Herpetoculturists, P.O. Box 1131, Lakeside, CA 92040.

WHAT ABOUT REGULATIONS?!

There has been a trend for many cities and even states to draft various laws or ordinances to restrict or prohibit the keeping of large monitor lizards (also iguanas and tegus). Various agencies and organizations support such regulations, normally under the guise that the public needs to be protected from the "potential danger" of such animals. Most of these regulations arise from a persistent bias against reptiles which permeates the attitudes of many people concerning these wonderful animals.

Considering the fact that dogs and cats actually present a greater threat to the public welfare, these laws would seem unfairly applied. Remember, too, that it is not possible for any reptile to ever contract rabies! Certainly, many other things in everyday life constitute a greater threat than reptiles, such as automobiles, electrical appliances, cooking gas, alcohol, tobacco, firearms, and sometimes, unfortunately, our fellow human beings.

In the case of monitor lizards, and particularly, savannah monitors, there is a very low probability of a severe or life-threatening situation ever arising. The author is unaware of any fatalities caused by monitor lizards in the U.S. over the last 10 years (or at all, frankly). Irresponsible owners of monitor lizards probably cause a lot more damage to the case for the captive maintenance of these animals than the animals themselves. Sound knowledge of the behavior of these lizards and a strict adherence to the recommendations of responsible herpetological organizations, like the AFH, can virtually eliminate any potential danger from these animals. The author believes that any problems associated with the ownership of any large lizard, particularly monitor lizards, can be handled in a responsible manner, without perpetuating misunderstanding, and without endangering the rights of herpetoculturists interested in these lizards.

NONETHELESS....
Before purchasing any monitor lizard, savannah or otherwise, it would be wise to check city, state, etc. regulations for any ordinances or other laws pertaining to the ownership of these lizards. Besides the various officials of the agencies involved with such enforcement, good sources of information are local herpetological organizations. It does not pay to be heedless of such laws or you could find yourself in a very unpleasant position, and you could gain a considerable amount of unwanted notoriety. If local officials contact state fish and game and/or federal fish and wildlife officers, you could be in for one of the most horrendous times of your life! In addition, your beloved pet will probably be confiscated.

Large savannah monitors can be quite a handful, but captive-raised animals tend to be docile. Agencies that aim to restrict the private ownership of savannah monitors have a biased position unsupported by statistical data. A better case could be made to ban the ownership of dogs. Photo by Robert Mailloux.

Selecting a Savannah Monitor

Selection of a lizard is a critical first step to owning a savannah monitor, and it will determine the course of your future relationship with the animal. When selecting any reptile, including a savannah monitor, choose only a healthy animal. Forget about saving any sick looking lizard in a pet store; sick reptiles virtually always DIE. Usually if a monitor lizard looks very ill, it has progressed to the point of no return, and you will almost certainly set yourself up for real disappointment. Don't waste your money and time, get a healthy animal and start off right.

WHAT TO AVOID

It is generally a good idea to avoid the purchase of any aggressive adult savannah monitor (2 or more feet long). Savannah monitors of this size are quite strong and will be a challenge to pick up and handle. Most will attempt to bite. Additionally, many of these initially aggressive animals will probably never become tame, even with frequent handling. It has been this author's experience, that many such savannah monitors, though seemingly healthy looking when purchased, are in fact quite stressed. They may eventually refuse to eat, and their psychological and physiological stress will depress their immune responses. When this happens, various disease symptoms may become apparent, and there is a good chance the lizard may end up dying of some sickness or other.

Avoid any lizard, large or small, wild-caught or captive-born that looks unhealthy in any way. These usually refuse to eat and will look starved. They will have low body weight, will often appear dehydrated, and will generally have a "skin and bones" appearance. They often have loose skin and sunken eyes. They will seem sluggish and generally not alert. They will often be too lethargic to flick their tongues in investigation.

SELECTING A HEALTHY SAVANNAH MONITOR

When available, the best choice for a savannah monitor is a captive-raised animal which has a healthy appearance, is active and alert, and even appears a bit extroverted (not to be confused with aggressive). In this case, the size of the lizard is not too important. If it shows good, exuberant health and calm behavior that is reasonably normal, it will be a good candidate as a "pet" and may even have potential for breeding. Of course, such animals should eat very readily.

The second best choice are imported young and apparently healthy savannah monitors. These should be alert, active, and be in "good flesh" (i.e., a bit "chubby" but not obese). Animals that have a "skin and bones" appearance or that are badly scratched or otherwise injured should be avoided. The vent/cloacal area should be clean and not have any wet or dry caked stool clinging to it. The belly should also be clean. Do not confuse normal shedding skin as a sign of bad health. The eyes should be round and clear. Healthy monitors readily flick their tongues when disturbed and when they walk around. A healthy young savannah monitor will be rather "squirmy" when picked up, but will usually calm down with frequent handling. Very young savannah monitors will sometimes defecate when first picked up, but this unpleasant habit will usually disappear with time and frequent handling. It can be a very satisfying experience to raise a baby savannah monitor to adulthood and these will often be excellent reptile pets.

ACCLIMATION

Acclimation (acclimatization) is when an organism becomes habituated to a different, usually abnormal, climate or environment. It is often used to describe an animal attempting to adjust to artificial or captive conditions. Whether your newly obtained savannah monitor acclimates or not depends upon the housing, maintenance, temperature, and nutritional conditions in which it is kept as well as its state of health when acquired. Furthermore, an individual lizard's "psychological profile" will play a major role in its ability to acclimate.

When your monitor is brought home, it will need some time to adjust to its new environment. This can take several weeks, and some animals will seem very stressed and may hide and fail to feed for the first few days or even weeks. Wild-caught specimens will usually puff up, hiss, and possibly swat their tails at you. Captive-raised animals usually fare better, but even they might not eat until adjusted.

Avoid moving or walking too closely and/or quickly towards the new animal or it may attempt to flee and run into the walls of its cage, possibly causing damage to its snout. It is important to provide a monitor with a shelter to hide in during this initial acclimation period. If you fail to allow the new animal to adjust, it may become stressed. This can inhibit the immune system and, more noticeably, its appetite. Establish a regular maintenance and feeding schedule during this time. Keep as much distance between you and the animal's enclosure as possible for the first few weeks. Offer it food every one to two days, until it begins to feed regularly. Some herpetoculturists advocate the use of an electrolyte solution like Gatorade®, instead of water during this period.

Within a few weeks or so, the animal should be eating regularly and gaining weight. In savannah monitors, weight loss is usually apparent around the hips and tail. A healthy animal has a rounded tail, and the hips are virtually indiscernible. When the animal is eating, showing some weight gain, does not appear overly stressed, and (with non-adult animals) is beginning to grow, you can work towards establishing a modicum of a pet-owner relationship.

It should be understood that a certain percentage of savannah monitors will probably not adjust well to captivity. Large wild-caught adults are particularly prone to this reaction. Occasionally, with early recognition and treatment (i.e., administering electrolyte therapy, high energy supplements, like Nutri-Cal®, etc.), you may be able to revitalize them, but this can be particularly difficult if the animal is aggressive towards you. Chances are that these animals will continue to be a problem and will require a considerable amount of time and effort. They will probably continue to suffer various effects from stress and eventually, despite all your efforts, fail to thrive and die. Do not give up if you are not successful the first time, but definitely avoid sick or inactive monitors as they will nearly always die.

An example of a newly imported Burundi Nile monitor which should be avoided by a prospective buyer. This animal is thin, sluggish and can barely keep its eyes open. It would require a certain amount of veterinary treatment to have this animal survive in captivity. Photo by Robert Mailloux.

Housing and General Maintenance

There are several things to consider before selecting a cage or enclosure for your savannah monitor. Because savannah monitors can grow quite rapidly in their initial year or two of life, it is important not to obtain an enclosure that may eventually become too small. For young specimens, all glass tanks with a locking screen top are available in many pet stores and can be a reasonably good choice. These are easy to find, easy to clean and provide a good view of your lizard. Purchase one as large as possible, because your monitor will definitely grow "into it." Certainly, a 30 or 55 gallon tank would not be too small to start. If you truly wish to be economical, then purchase as large a tank as you can; the space will eventually not go to waste. If you are planning to raise other young specimens in the future, then it might be wise to obtain several different sized tanks to cycle through the various sized monitors and economize a bit on space. Certainly, common sense should prevail. When your savannah monitor reaches a length of about 3 feet (1 meter, adult size), it will probably be necessary to get a larger enclosure than most glass tanks could easily provide. There are several choices to be had. One choice is to have a large cage custom built. There are also now a number of high quality enclosure manufacturers that specialize in reptile housing. Local reptile stores can be a good sources for these cages. One can also find enclosure manufacturers in the advertising section of various herpetological publications.

Finally, one enclosure this author has used successfully over the years for very large, tame monitors is the largest of the "take-apart" indoor galvanized steel dog kennels having three sides covered with a plastic painter's tarp (to reduce drafts). When buying these indoor kennels, the major "trick" is to obtain one with very small space between the bars, so your monitor cannot escape. If it can get its head through the bars, normally the rest of the body can follow (or it may get dangerously stuck). Useful ones can be found in many of the larger general purpose pet stores.

Generally, a cage for a monitor should be one and a half to two or more times the snout to vent length of the lizard, two thirds to one times the length of the animal in width, and one to one and half times the length of the animal in height (with height, be sure the lizard cannot peer over the top). Again, the larger the enclosure you can provide, the better. Homemade cages can be constructed of wood, with a built-in glass (or better, plexiglass, although this can scratch more easily) front. The top should have screening to provide ventilation and to allow for placement of various lights. Screen sides are not recommended. The type of screen used must be resistant to monitor claws and must be attached very securely to the cage. Hardware cloth and plastic coated welded wire are likely to be the best. The door(s) can be in the front, sides or the top. This author prefers to reach down to pick up a monitor (so long as the cage is not more than three feet high) rather than coming towards it from the front, especially with frigntened or aggressive specimens. Hinged locking doors are to be preferred to doors that slide up (the potential to "guillotine" must be considered), but doors that slide to one side are usable. Probably, the best solution for caging the larger species of monitors is to provide them with small rooms or room-sized enclosures with some sort of drainage in the floor for easy cleaning.

Remember, any cage you use must be secure against escape. Savannah monitors have amazing strength at any size and really big ones can seem almost herculean at times, so all screening must be firmly secured to the top and must be resistant to shredding by their claws. All plexiglass or glass must be secure and thick enough to be shatterproof. The doors of cages will need to be secured with some kind of locking mechanism. Savannah monitors can be amazingly "clever" and they have good memories when they devise escape methods. So, should a savannah monitor somehow manage to escape from its enclosure, an escape-proof, locked room will be an added security. The additional security of a locked room will mean that your neighbors will not receive unwanted visits from your pet, should it somehow escape from its enclosure. Should the "unexpected" occur, try to find out how it is escaping, or you will be continually confronted with a lizard on the loose!

CAGE LOCATION, SUBSTRATES, AND CLEANING

Savannah monitors grow rather large so a reasonably sized room with adequate open space to allow easy maintenance and handling of the animal will be required. An adult savanna monitor in a cluttered room can cause the inadvertent toppling of furniture while being handled. These lizards do not hesitate to flail and will also grab anything within reach. Extracting your lizard from a prize piece of clothing or the drapery can be no small feat. The room should be kept locked when you are not inside, and the lock should be tamper-proof, both against inside and outside residents. The door should always be kept closed. Inspect the room and patch all holes to ensure that any savannah monitor that escapes its enclosure (which normally should not occur, if the cage is properly made and kept locked) will be unable to leave the room. Savannah monitors are notorious escape artists and can squeeze into and under amazingly small openings or if large and powerful enough, can enlarge a smaller opening. It is common for these lizards to get into the walls via some overlooked opening or hole. Coaxing them out of such a place can be extremely trying and difficult. A savannah monitor which escapes to the outside will surely get you and itself into plenty of trouble! Don't let it happen.

Providing your monitor with a fancily decorated cage would almost certainly require a room-sized enclosure. Most herpetoculturists opt not to do this. Simple, and easily maintained conditions will need to be the norm for these lizards, especially the adults. Plants as decorations will be pretty much impossible unless one has the space and conditions to maintain shrubs and trees. However, some savannah monitors enjoy a good climb, so it is a good idea to provide some sort of climbing branch or pole.

GROUND MEDIA
Ideal ground media for maintaining large monitors are newspaper or brown butcher's paper. They are inexpensive, easy to obtain and replace, and make cleaning the cage very economical and simple. Some herpetoculturists like to use some type of wood chips or bark, (but DO NOT USE CEDAR which can be toxic) or pine shavings as a substrate. Others will use a fine to medium pea gravel. This is acceptable, but beware of the lizard accidentally ingesting any of this material when it feeds, as this can cause serious problems. Others may opt to use an "Astro-turf" or similar artificial grass mat. These latter options may be more aesthetic, but the owner must always remember that savannah monitors (as well as all other monitor species) defecate frequently and in often incredibly large amounts. Additionally, their stools often contain much wet and semi-solid material and typically have a very unpleasant odor. Unless one has a monitor which regularly defecates in a large water container when placed in the cage (a common pattern), one should select easily replaceable ground media. Another ground medium which has been used successfully, particularly with younger savannah monitors, are rabbit or alfalfa pellets.

SHELTERS
Most savannah monitors prefer to have some sort of shelter, especially when they are young. Some, instead of using shelters will bury themselves under the substrate. As a general rule, a monitor will usually establish better if it is provided with a place where it can feel safe and secure. Easily obtainable and inexpensive shelters can be made from inverted cardboard boxes with a hole cut in the front. Remove these as they become dirty. More permanent and aesthetic shelters can be purchased such as bark, cork sections or the plastic or ceramic shelters now offered by many reptile stores. The latter are especially useful because they can be easily cleaned. For larger specimens, use specially built wooden shelters or the enclosed cat litter boxes. Shelters can play a significant role in reducing captive stress, yet they are an often overlooked aspect of vivarium design.

TEMPERATURE
Monitor lizards are all Old World reptiles which come largely from tropical and subtropical areas. All the subspecies of the savannah monitor come from a habitat that is, normally, very hot and rather dry in the day, to somewhat warm, albeit cooler, at night. Their ranges include most of the semi-desert and savannah regions of sub-Saharan Africa (except the West Cape). This climate has a modicum of seasonal rainfall, at least in some places, and in the far south can be downright cold

A well designed savannah monitor enclosure with a shelter, heat source and water dish. Photo by Glen Carlzen.

A savannah monitor basking on a "hot rock" in a custom-made enclosure. Photo by Glen Carlzen.

at times. Savannah monitors that live where it can get cool may have a short seasonal hibernation period.

With the above in mind, one should provide a daytime temperature of 85-90°F (29-32°C). At night, the temperature can safely be allowed to drop 10-15°F (about 6-8°C). Additionally, one should place a thermostatically controlled heating pad (connected to a thermostat) to provide a warm area.

Keep track of the temperature in your monitor's enclosure room. At the very least, use a high/low thermometer that will indicate the maximum and minimum temperatures for each day. These thermometers are usually manually reset on a daily basis. One of the most recommended type of thermometers, are the electronic digital thermometers with an alarm and a sensor (when temperature is too high or low) and a program for giving daily high/low temperature readings. With one setting, you can obtain a continuous read-out of the room's temperature. By switching the setting, you can get a read-out for a sensor placed in the basking area or some other desired spot. Knowing what the daily temperature fluctuations are will be helpful in monitoring your lizard's daily health.

HEATING SYSTEMS AND METHODS

Space heaters or room heaters. A somewhat economical method of keeping a room warm is to use an electrical heater, such as a space heater, an electric radiator, or a ceramic electric heater. This works well for people keeping animals which have similar temperature requirements. The use of these devices can have its problems, however. The major problem is overheating. The use of a backup thermostat on the heater, coupled to an alarm on your thermometer (as described above) can usually go a long way to preventing this problem, so long as you ensure that both systems are working. Always buy space heaters with safety features to reduce the risk of fire. Additionally, placement can be a problem. If the heater is in a spot where there is a cool draft, it may misread "local" coolness for the average room temperature and thereby, overheat the room. Temperature gradients will also form in the room. Thus, it will be warmer near the ceiling than on the floor. This must be remembered when placing cages in the room at differing heights. Also, beware of potential fire hazard when placing your space heater. It should be in an open area, away from furniture, curtains or other flammable products. Keep on top of heater placement, thermostats and thermometers and you should be able to avoid tragedy.

Hot rocks. These can be very useful as a heat source for small monitors, but they should be carefully monitored for overheating. Subtle thermal burns on the ventral (belly) skin can result when lizards bask on overheating (temperatures of 105 degrees or greater) hot rocks. Frequent monitoring of the hot rock should prevent any problem. The surface temperature of the hot rock should be 85-95°F (29-35°C). Placing a flat rock on top of the hot rock will often diffuse the heat down to a satisfactory level. As your monitor grows larger, you will have to consider an alternative source of heat such as "pig blankets".

Incandescent lights. Incandescent floodlights or spotlights (75 watts and up depending on the temperature) can be used to keep a savannah monitor warm. Just remember to use a thermometer to assure that the basking site is within the desirable range (85-95°F). In large, tall enclosures, infra-red bulbs (like the GE infra-red reflector 115-125 V/250 watt type, that are used in fast food places to keep French fries warm) are highly recommended because they can be kept on at night, if necessary, without any detriment to the animal (i.e., it is not in perpetual daylight). Whatever type of bulb you decide on, ensure that the fixture and the bulb do not directly contact the animal in any way. Reptiles are not normally exposed to heat of such potentially damaging temperatures in the wild and often do not seem to notice burn injuries as they are occurring. The resulting burns can be very traumatic and even fatal. After the bulb has been on about an hour, measure the temperature of the basking area directly under the bulb and to some distance out to ensure this area is not too hot. Again, as with space heaters, make sure that nothing flammable can contact or be ignited by the bulb, to avoid a fire.

Heating pads. Subtank reptile and standard heating pads can be useful for providing heat to savannah monitors, though they may be too small for some larger species or specimens.

Fiberglass heating pads or pig blankets. These devices are sold in feed stores and specialized reptile stores. Many herpetoculturists claim that these are among the best heating units for large reptiles. Basically, they are moderately large (at least three feet by one foot), ridged fiberglass enclosed units that provide high surface heat over a broad area. When used with the thermostat that can be special ordered from the manufacturer, these are ideal for savannah monitors and, of course, other large monitor species.

LIGHTING

Most animals require circadian (24 hour) light/dark cycle, and savannah monitors are no exception. Provide monitors with 12 to 14 hours of daylight, using when possible, a combination of artificial and natural light. Many herpetoculturists will use a Vita Lite® or some similar full-spectrum light for their animals. This author has also used regular fluorescent bulbs with as much success. It is possible, though, that subtle benefits can be derived from lights that simulate natural daylight, so the use of full-spectrum bulbs should be considered. Unlike some herpetoculturists, this author does not advocate the use of any black or ultra-violet light as the potential for harm (especially to the eyes and skin: see Ross, 1990), via excess or misuse, may exceed any benefit. With proper diet, possibly including some modicum of supplementation, your monitor should not require UV light to synthesize vitamin D3. If the design of your vivarium allows it (some herpetoculturists have specially designed accesses to outdoor vivaria), provide regular access to natural, unfiltered sunlight though this is not required for the maintenance of monitors in captivity.

MAINTENANCE

The living quarters of your savannah monitor will need regular hygienic maintenance. Remove feces and other waste products as well as any soiled substrate. Clean the cage with some sort of mild disinfectant, at least once a week. The author prefers a dilute solution of Nolvolsan-S (chlorihexidine)®, but dilute sodium hypochlorite bleach (5% common household bleach solution such as Clorox®) also works well. NEVER USE PHENOLIC COMPOUNDS SUCH AS LYSOL®, AS RESIDUES COULD BE TOXIC! Be sure to remove all traces of disinfectant. The water container should be washed, disinfected, rinsed, and refilled with fresh water at least once a week. If the water vessel is large enough, monitors may climb into it and soak. In the process, many lizards will defecate, so remove such soiled water as soon as possible, disinfect the container, and replace the water.

EQUIPMENT

A very useful piece of equipment for dealing with large monitors are thick, long cuffed, leather gloves, such as those used by welders or hedge-cutters. Another tool this author has used on occasion is a broom handle. Sometimes moderately large monitors can be induced to cling to the broom handle and thereby, with modest restraint, be moved about. The author has used this technique with some success largely with moderately difficult lizards, especially the arboreal species, but some savannah monitors can be "taught" this trick. A modest-sized, fairly heavy snake hook turned sideways, can serve equally well. Remember too, that with a modicum of care, monitors can if necessary, be lifted by the tail for very short periods and distances. This works especially well with smaller animals, without risk of breaking the tail, because these lizards do not have caudal autotomy (the "self-fracturing" tail possessed by most lizard families). Avoid doing this with really "squirmy" or aggressive animals.

An adult savannah monitor in a custom-made enclosure. The shelter was removed. The primary heat source is a "hot rock" type of heater. Photo by Ned Gilmore.

Feeding

Healthy savannah monitors of any size will readily feed and it is usually a bad sign when they do not. Sometimes adults will fast during their breeding season (which is normally in the late fall), and the author has occasionally observed this from time to time. However, the author has also observed this to occur in some long term captives in the late winter (January-March). If they are in good health and not thin, short fasts can be tolerated without concern, but keep a close eye on the situation, and especially be on the lookout for dehydration.

Most adult and juvenile monitors of about one foot or more in total length will readily devour pre-killed rodents (all commercially-bred types) or baby chickens. They are also quite fond of eggs and an **occasional** egg can be given, but only use egg yolks or embryonated eggs obtainable in health food markets. The whites of non-embryonated eggs contain avidin which, in excess, can induce a biotin (vitamin B4) deficiency. This problem manifests itself as a generalized "diffuse" muscular weakness. There is also a great risk of *Salmonella* infection when feeding raw eggs. A safe option is to offer cooked eggs. While chicken parts are also readily eaten by savannah monitors, be aware that raw chicken may be contaminated with *Salmonella*, and is best avoided. If you feed them chicken make sure it has been cooked.

DIETS FOR HATCHLING AND SMALL MONITORS

Very young savannah monitors (i.e., under one foot) can be fed live crickets, earthworms ("nightcrawlers"), the so-called "king mealworms" (*Zoophobias*), and baby mice (both "pinkies" and "fuzzies," depending on the size of your animal) The author has had **excellent** success using canned cat food, especially poultry flavors. Use a good brand of canned cat food to insure adequate nutrition. Occasionally, canned cat food can be offered to adult monitors, especially those recovering from illness. The only problem you can sometimes experience with canned cat food is that your lizard may have a somewhat loose stool. This can normally be corrected by alternating feedings with prey animals such as fuzzies or just weaned mice, between cat food feedings.

SIZE OF PREY & LIVE VS. PREKILLED FOOD

The size of prey that can be offered a monitor can be judged by the size of the head of your animal and its gape. Normally, your animal will not attempt to devour anything it judges too large to easily swallow. For example, a baby savannah monitor will be unable to eat an adult mouse and will usually not attempt to do so or will cease trying very quickly. Some monitors can dismantle a large prey item with their claws and mouths and devour it in pieces, but very young animals will normally avoid doing this. There are rare times when a savannah monitor will eat a prey item that is too large, and this usually will be regurgitated sometime thereafter. This does not normally cause harm to your animal, but monitor vomit is among the most incredibly foul smelling materials in the world! It is rare that even a full grown adult savannah monitor will be able to eat a guinea pig or large rat (at least not without "disassembly," which can be unaesthetic and messy), but nearly any other "domesticated" rodent will be usable (e.g., pre-killed hamsters, mice, small rats, and the like). In the wild, savannah monitors were found to eat baby tortoises, grasshoppers, crickets and their relatives, millipedes, centipedes, caterpillars, snails, beetles, scorpions, frogs, and lizard eggs. Wild specimens also will eat small rodents, baby birds, and small lizards, when the opportunity arises.

Prekilled prey (except insects and "nightcrawlers") can and should be offered to savannah monitors. This minimizes the suffering of the prey animal and eliminates the possibility of your monitor suffering a nasty bite by the prey. This author has seen some rather severe damage inflicted by rodents and this can be easily avoided by using dead prey. Also, prekilled animals can be easily placed within the cage or removed if not eaten. There are several ways to kill rodents. Perhaps the most humane way is to break the animals neck by either grabbing the tail and swiftly striking the back of the head against the edge of a table or holding the animal using a wood dowel firmly behind the head where it meets the neck and firmly pulling the tail (this is especially effective for mice, but not recommended for adult rats). A humane method for mass euthanasia, is to place the rodents in a container that can be sealed with a piece of dry ice for about 15 minutes.

It has been suggested that prey items should be offered soon after their removal from the rearing cages. Apparently, the residual food in the prey animal's digestive tract will help supply the monitor with vitamins (especially Vitamin C) and the like. Vitamin C from such "gut contents" has been suggested as having some efficacy in preventing stomatitis (mouthrot) and maintaining the integrity of your monitor's skin (Frye, 1981, 1991).

FEEDING SCHEDULES AND REGIMENS

If all other conditions are adequate, the growth of your savannah monitor will be directly related to its feeding regimen. The growth rate for a savannah monitor will be greatest during the first 2 to 3 years with much occurring during the first year and a half. When sexual maturity occurs in savannah monitors is difficult to say, but it has been noted that this may occur in *V. olivaceus* at about the end of their second year, or the beginning of their third year (apparently similarly for *V. bengalensis*) (Auffenberg, 1988). Both of the above species are approximately the same size as a savannah monitor or a bit bigger. When growth slows down, it is best to reduce the feeding regimen. Remember that if you are fortunate enough to get your monitors to breed, or if you buy a gravid female, that the feeding schedule should be increased to assure that egg-laying females maintain adequate weight.

Hatchlings to about 1 foot (total length). Feed monitors this size one to four small (fuzzy to young adult) mice every two to three days. Adjust the size of rodents as the animal grows larger. One can also occasionally offer them 1 1/2 to 4 tablespoons of canned cat food per week (this seems small, but it is a richer diet). King mealworms, crickets and earthworms can also be offered. Crickets can be utilized as a means to "exercise" young monitors, and it can be quite an amusing spectacle to watch them chasing crickets all about their cages.

1-foot to adult size (app. 3 feet total length). Feed animals of this size one to four adult mice twice a week. 1-footers can be given 1/2 to 3/4 can of canned cat food per week, but do not overdo it. Rodents will provide the best diet, but canned cat food will prove useful for convalescing lizards and when your rodent supplier is temporarily out of stock. Adjust the diet if animals appear overweight or too thin.

Adults (3 feet or more total length). Feed lizards of this age twice a week and adjust to prevent obesity. Some large savannah monitors can be real gluttons and eat as much as ten or more adult mice per week. Larger savannah monitors can also be offered small weaned rats. If savannah monitors are not given the opportunity to exercise, they will get quite fat so be careful not to overfeed. If your lizard looks in good health and is not getting too fat or, more rarely, too thin, your regimen is probably adequate. Some experimentation is recommended here and at the other ages as well, based on type of food, ambient temperature, and amount of activity. Use your own judgment based on the above guidelines, at all times. Keeping records of how much and when you fed, and how the animal responded, can be useful and handy references, especially if you plan to raise more young savannah monitors later.

STUNTING

If your monitor is only infrequently fed or offered small amounts of food during its first year or so, it can become stunted. Monitor lizards have high metabolisms for reptiles and maintaining animals on minimal diets may have serious consequences. It may take much longer to raise an animal to maturity and it may very likely never reach its full potential size. Be responsible. If you are not willing to adequately feed a savannah monitor, do not buy one. A reptile which requires less maintenance, such as many of the species of snakes may be better suited to your lifestyle.

THE PROPER METHOD FOR FEEDING A MONITOR

When under a foot in total length, monitors can be fed without any particular heed to special precautions, other than some care when placing or removing the food. But once a larger size is achieved, a herpetoculturist will need to practice safe feeding procedures to avoid injury to himself! What follows are sound feeding practices to avoid the possibility of serious accidental bites.

1. Keep only one lizard per cage. This is a good idea anyway because monitors are known to inflict serious injuries upon each other during a fight, and the potential for squabbling is fairly high, especially among same sex individuals.

2. Have the food within your easy reach (in case you need to remove it) and be sure you know where the monitor is prior to opening the door of the cage. Obviously, the lizard should not be near the door. If it is near the door, open the door and use a snake stick or blunt broom handle to encourage the lizard to move away. Then, using a pair of long forceps or tongs, introduce the food to some area at a reasonably good distance from the door. NEVER HOLD OR DANGLE THE FOOD ITEM IN YOUR BARE HAND OR ENCOURAGE THE MONITOR TO GRAB THE FOOD FROM YOUR UNPROTECTED HAND! Fingers and hands will become amazingly "prey-like" under such circumstances. The resulting injuries could require a trip to the emergency clinic!

3. If the lizard fails to eat the food (within 12 hours, usually), and it needs to be removed, encourage the monitor to leave the food site, and push the food towards the door of the cage with tongs or long forceps. You can use your hand only if the lizard is nowhere near the food, but the use of tongs or forceps at all times is to be preferred. Remember, monitor lizards can move incredibly fast when they desire to do so. It is a good idea to put a board or some other shield between you and the lizard when removing food. A very good shield can be made by attaching a handle to a section of plexiglass (size will depend on the dimensions of the cage) so you can see the lizard at all times.

WATER

While savannah monitors hail from somewhat arid climates, they still require water, and they drink regularly. Other monitor species may actually spend some time swimming in water (e.g., *V. niloticus*, *V. salvator*, and *V. indicus*). Captive monitors should regularly have access to a heavy, large container of water. However, care must be taken not to overhumidify, especially do not allow the cage to become completely and continuously wet. Most monitors will enjoy a good soak on occasion. Soaking in warm water will also encourage monitors to defecate. Remember never to allow feces-contaminated water to sit for extended periods, because disease-causing microbes could multiply there. Disinfect any such water container prior to restoring it. In addition to maintaining a clean water container, never allow savannah monitors to remain in soggy cages for extended periods of time and make sure there is adequate ventilation in the enclosure.

Grooming

While it is not possible to "groom" a savannah monitor in the sense of a dog or cat, certain things can be done to facilitate handling and benefit the health of your lizard.

1. Claw trimming:
Because most setups for your monitor will not provide a surface that is rough enough or a space large enough to allow your lizard to wear down its claws, regular trimming of the claws will probably be necessary. Monitors will naturally develop very sharp pointed claws that can inflict such a significant amount of superficial damage to your skin that handling them without some protection can result in multiple small puncture wounds, deep scratches and excruciating pain. If the claws are kept trimmed, your monitor can be handled without damage to yourself or your clothes.

Trimming the claws of adult monitors will require two (or even better, three) people and good illumination. The person handling the lizard (wear gloves) should hold it with both hands. One hand should encircle the neck and area above the forelegs. The other hand should encircle the area above the hindlegs. With a very large animal, one person should hold onto the front end and the other onto the hip area. The tail should be stabilized against one's body or a firm flat surface. Remember that monitors will whip and thrash their tails. Hold the monitor firmly and tilt it vertically or sideways, so that the lizard's "belly" is towards the person trimming the claws. Beware, some monitors will also take this opportunity to defecate on you!

Trim the claws as per the following procedure:

a. Use rubbing alcohol or Betadine ® and apply via a cotton swab or gauze pad to the claws and the surrounding areas of the "hand" or foot to be trimmed. This will disinfect this area.

b. Hold the lizard's finger or toe at the base of the claw and examine carefully under a good light. Clip the point where you can see no blood vessels or anything else. In other words, you should be able to see (more or less) clear through the claw without encountering any other tissues. Use nail clippers or dog/cat nail clippers to cut the point and then file any sharp edges with a nail file or emery board. Be very meticulous because sometimes the claws can be very dark (especially in large animals), and blood vessels can be very hard to see. When in doubt, cut only the sharp tip. If you accidently "nick" any blood vessels or other nail tissues and the lizard bleeds, wipe the claw with some disinfectant and dip the bleeding tip into corn starch or Kwik Stop ® (be sure to have these ready just in case). An alternative to doing this yourself is to hire the services of skilled personnel of pet shops (if they are willing) that deal heavily in birds. They trim bird claws regularly, and the

A captive-raised three year old male savannah monitor (*Varanus e. exanthematicus*). Careful initial selection, regular handling and trimmed nails are essential if one desires a tame pet savannah monitor.

Caution must be used when offering prekilled rodents by hand. With larger monitors, the use of tongs or simply tossing the prekilled prey at one end of the enclosure is recommended. Photo by Chris Estep.

process is quite similar. Some veterinarians are capable of providing this service as well. Remember, clip only the pointed tip, as cutting the claw's base can result in much more serious bleeding, and the risk of infection is increased. With some practice, anyone can become reasonably good at performing this necessary task.

2. General grooming:

Keeping your monitor clean is essential for its long-term good health. Many savannah monitors enjoy a good "soak" so it is appropriate to offer the lizard a large container of warm water at least every couple of weeks. Large plastic tubs are recommended for this purpose. For very large animals, some people simply place their animals in the bathtub since it is convenient to fill and drain (ensure that the water temperature is only warm, not hot to the touch). Be sure that the water level just barely covers the back of the animal and check on the lizard frequently. After soaking, you can frequently remove any loose skin still clinging to your savannah monitor. Be sure to adequately dry off your monitor to prevent any sudden chill, and thereby, the risk of respiratory ailments. As a general rule, the use of bathtubs is not recommended for this purpose. Large tubs in a securely locked enclosure are preferable because this method will prevent any risk of escape. Sanitation should be another consideration for avoiding the use of bathtubs.

Careful initial selection of a monitor and regular handling will be necessary to develop a good pet/owner relationship. Juvenile monitors are often initially flighty but many settle down as they get older. Nile monitors can vary greatly in personality and initial selection of a calm animal can be critical with this species. Photo by Chris Estep.

Developing a "Pet/Owner" Relationship

The main point to keep in mind when developing a "pet/owner" relationship with your savannah monitor is to be totally non-threatening to your lizard. Certainly, this type of relationship can be developed far more easily with captive-raised adults (which are probably already pets) or young animals. When a captive savannah monitor habituates to humans, it will no longer show any desire to run away or attack. This means the animal will be calm when approached and will allow itself to be handled and carried. Such animals will often allow themselves to be petted or otherwise touched. An established monitor will normally approach you when you are bringing it food and will accept food offered from forceps. It should be relatively calm when moved about to other parts of your home. Basically, a pet savannah monitor loses its fear of humans and can then be one of the best and most rewarding reptile pets. To achieve this relationship, frequent and regular interaction will be required.

After acclimation, you can begin short periods of interaction. Keep any other pets (especially cats and dogs) out of sight and smell of your new lizard during your initial taming and handling sessions, as these can frighten your monitor. Bear in mind that savannah monitors will normally not tolerate extended periods of handling or petting. Never take your lizard outside or in public places because your monitor may suddenly become frightened, and you may lose it. Also, you do not want to risk frightening the general public and thereby add to the notion that herpetoculturists are irresponsible.

Various herpetoculturists have differing approaches to working with monitors. You could begin by scratching a monitor behind the head or on the back of its neck, then progress to lightly stroking its sides. You might then slowly pick up the lizard and then place it back in the cage a few times. With small animals, it is a good technique to often take them out of the cage and allow them to travel from one hand to another while trying to persuade them to do so as calmly as possible. Almost certainly, when trying this technique, your lizard will attempt to run away, but if caught and persuaded after several attempts to move slowly from one hand to the next, your savannah monitor will calm down and do what you want it to do. This is the initial step in getting your lizard familiar with being picked up and handled. Remember that trimmed claws will make the handling of your lizard easier on you. If you stroke the back of its neck and sides, this can often enhance your lizard's favorable response to your handling. Usually after a period of a few weeks, you will probably notice that your monitor is becoming calmer. Its behavior will guide you in deciding the extent that it can be left out of its cage and in a familiar area.

The degree of tameness you get with your monitor will largely depend on the amount of time and effort you invest in interacting with it. This author has seen savannah monitors so tame that they will lie quite still and allow many strangers to observe and even touch them. The author has had several that were "dog-tame", and one which would allow him to pose it for humorous holiday snapshots.

The use of a small dog or cat harness combined with a leash can be very useful for preventing a tame savannah monitor from suddenly darting off at a time or place where this would not be convenient. Harnesses can also be used to train and control your lizard when allowing it to roam about the house.

SAVANNAH MONITOR PERSONALITIES

If you encounter enough savannah monitors, you will soon discover that they can exhibit a wide variety of personalities. Some are extroverted and even appear to enjoy the company of humans, some will be nervous, shy, and possibly even scared. Some monitors will be feisty and asocial, lashing their tails and generally acting a bit snappy. Thus, not all savannah monitors will be great pets. Some are, at best, tolerant of humans and will only make good display animals. If one animal turns out to not be such a great pet, perhaps you might consider acquiring another (given the space). A couple of savannah monitors are not much more time consuming or difficult to keep than one.

It is important for readers to be able to recognize when a monitor lizard is angry and the stereotypical threat/display behaviors that accompany this reaction. Sometimes an angry monitor will turn toward a person with its mouth wide open. This is normally followed by a sudden lunge if you get too close! At other times the lizard will hiss loudly, inflate its throat, and produce a pronounced curve in the neck by bowing its head (this is called a raised "roach"). This may be accompanied by rather violent twitching, curling and possibly lashing of the tail. When monitor lizards are angry or afraid, they can be amazingly aggressive, and handling the animal at that time may result in a serious bite. Injuries by large specimens may require stitches. Many monitors lash their tails as a threat, including savannah monitors, and a "smack" by any species can be rather unpleasant. Savannah monitors have very thick tails that actually feel like clubs. Finally, many monitors will readily defecate upon anyone who seizes and handles them when they are afraid. It should always be remembered that these animals can be formidable adversaries when they appear aggressive or afraid, but this is true for any large captive animal. Treat them with respect and enjoy their company.

Savannah monitors and other monitor species tend to undergo developmental changes in personality. Many babies tend to be a bit flighty, nervous, or even aggressive. Later, as they mature, a significant percentage will calm down, but some may become even more wary and aggressive.

An angry white-throated monitor (*Varanus e. albigularis*) ready to lash out with its tail. Photographed at the Norden Zoo by Mark Bayless.

A tame adult ornate Nile monitor (*Varanus niloticus ornatus*). Photo by Greg Naclerio.

Disorders and Diseases

Proper husbandry, with a maintenance schedule to assure good hygienic conditions, will help ensure that your savannah monitors live long and healthy lives. Most disease results from poor initial selection, improper or inadequate husbandry, poor diet, bad hygiene, or maladaptation. Remember, too, that if escape is even vaguely probable, it will occur, and if there is any way your lizard can injure itself, it frequently will do so after an escape. Observe your lizards, think about prevention and be ever on the look-out for potential trouble.

WHAT TO BE ON THE LOOK OUT FOR!

Try to catch any ailment early. Often, when captive monitors are so obviously ill that immediate attention is needed, a disease will have progressed to the point where it cannot usually be treated successfully by a veterinarian. Thus many lizards sick enough to merit a veterinarian's attention do not survive. To discover a possibility of disease early, develop a "quick-check" method which will eventually become automatic and will allow for the recognition of any disease or other disorder as early as possible. Check for:

a. **General responsiveness/alertness.** Is your savannah monitor acting in any way abnormal? Is it unusually sluggish? Is it not feeding?

b. **Breathing.** Does your monitor gape much of the time? Does it occasionally forcibly expel air? Does mucus collect at the edge of its mouth or nostrils?

c. **Mouth area.** Is there any apparent swelling along the rim of your lizards mouth when closed? Has any food, debris, or other foreign material accumulated along the rim of its mouth? Are any lumps visible along the upper and/or lower jaws?

d. **Eyes.** Do the eyes appear to be alert? Are they wide open or narrowed? Do the lids show any swelling? Are they unusually wet or dry? Any crust accumulating around them? Are they swollen shut? Do the eyes appear cloudy in any way?

e. **Body.** Any cuts, scratches, or swellings? Any skin disease, lumps, brownish or blackish areas, open or running sores? Swollen limbs? Any signs of paralysis? Does your monitor walk funny? Does the head tilt or is it otherwise held in an "abnormal" position?

f. **Hands and feet.** Are any toes or fingers swollen? Is the whole foot or hand swollen? Are there remains of shed skin clinging to the toes or fingers? Has a claw suddenly disappeared?

g. **Signs of watery stools.** Check for bloody stools. Are there any stains or smeared feces around the vent? Is the vent swollen? Does the animal have frequent, unusually watery stools? Has the animal failed to defecate or otherwise excrete for an unusually long time?

If you can answer yes to any of the above questions, your savannah monitor will probably need veterinary attention and/or some modification and improvement in husbandry.

VETERINARIANS

Finding a veterinarian with experience in the treatment of reptiles and other exotic animals can be a difficult problem. Veterinarians with no experience or knowledge about reptiles and/or herpetology, can at times do more harm than good. Check with local herpetological societies for information about veterinarians with knowledge of treating reptiles.

Barring this, or if you live in an area where there may be no experienced veterinarians, you might consider the purchase of a basic and well known reference work for herpetological medicine. One of the best known is Fredric L. Frye's: Biomedical and Surgical Aspects of Captive Reptile Husbandry (1981. VM Publishing Co.), which is now available in a new 2 volume edition from Krieger Publishing Co. (Melbourne, FL) or from TFH under the title: Reptile Care: An Atlas of Diseases and Treatments. The older edition can occasionally be purchased, but one must remember that some of the drug dosages may no longer be valid. Be that as it may, with the help of one (or more) of these references, and the willing cooperation of a local veterinarian, it is reasonable to presume that diagnosis and appropriate treatment of many reptile diseases can be accomplished. Several references of worth are:

1. Jacobson, Elliott R. and George V. Kollias (editors) 1988. Exotic Animals. Churchill Livingstone, NY. (Drug doses good).

2. Marcus, Leonard C. 1981. Veterinary Biology and Medicine of Captive Amphibians and Reptiles. Lea & Febiger, Philadelphia. (Provides some good background in some basic herpetology as well).

3. Ross, Richard A. and Gerald Marzec. 1984. The Bacterial Diseases of Reptiles. Institute For Herpetological Research, Stanford, CA.

4. Cooper, John E. and Oliphant F. Jackson (editors) 1981. Diseases of the Reptilia, 2 volumes. Academic Press, London, England.

COMMON DISORDERS AND DISEASES

a. **Thermal burns.** This usually results from improperly shielding your lizard from spotlights or other excessively warm heating devices. Superficial burns will eventually heal, but scarring may result. Serious burns will require veterinary care. Be sure to protect the animal from any direct contact with a heat lamp or spotlight. Monitor the temperatures of all hot rocks and similar such devices, modifying or removing those that are overheated.

b. **Nose rub** (rostral abrasion). This occurs when your monitor ceaselessly rubs its snout against screen mesh or hard surfaces. This happens because the animal is improperly housed (screening should be avoided for the sides of monitor cages). This behavior can also occur if the cage is too small or poorly designed. A monitor that rubs its snout is indicating that it does not like where it is for whatever reason (such as: the cage is too warm or cold, too bright, etc.). Sometimes the reason is not immediately obvious, for example, the animal may be trying to reach a patch of sunlight it has spotted in some inaccessible part of the room. Try to discover the reason the animal is unhappy and correct the problem. Additionally, you may need to cover up the areas with wire mesh to prevent further damage. Place your animal in conditions where these behaviors and the resulting traumas do not persist. Remember, if the monitor does not stop rubbing its snout, the trauma will become progressively worse. Early treatment with an antibiotic salve can help the wound heal and often with little scarring. In extreme cases, your lizard can cause such damage to its snout that the entire front is destroyed, and bone and teeth may actually be exposed! Catch and treat this problem early.

c. **Skin and foot infections.** If your monitor is kept in conditions that are too humid or wet (especially if hygiene is not the best), it could develop skin and toe infections. Extreme humid conditions are inappropriate for savannah monitors because they are native to areas with hot, dry climates. These infections appear as whitish or more commonly, brownish to blackish raised areas. The toes will usually swell as well and be stained as above. Put the animal on a dry surface (such as clean newspaper). Keep its enclosure scrupulously clean and dry and disinfect it as well. Apply topical antibiotics to the infected surfaces. Swollen toes may require veterinary treatment.

Another problem probably related to humidity, especially rapid and great changes in humidity, is that many savannah monitors may develop bizarre, reoccurring hind foot (usually, though front feet may also be involved in some animals) abscesses. These infections are peculiar because they will normally appear at about the same time of year, every year of the animal's life. This author has been told that this problem has been seen in some other lizards (such as desert iguanas, *Dipsosaurus dorsalis*) from arid climates, that are kept in more humid areas by herpetoculturists. These abscesses are time consuming to deal with and will require veterinary help in most cases. It helps to become experienced at treating this problem if your animal shows this syndrome. The author suspects it may be a form of stress induced by unfavorable climatological conditions, though not all savannah monitors will manifest this problem. Perhaps, the use of a dehumidifier (when excessively humid) may help prevent this problem.

PARASITES
External parasites
Ticks: If you obtain your animal from a good and reliable source, you will probably never see ticks on the surface of your savannah monitor, despite the fact that these lizards are attacked by several species in the wild. The author once obtained (rescued) a specimen from a pet store that harbored a tick. When it was "keyed out", it was found to be a native African tick that frequently attacks monitor lizards. The treatment for ticks is fairly easy. Apply some rubbing alcohol to the tick's surface (often several applications may be needed), and soon the irritated parasite will begin to withdraw its mouth parts from your lizard. At that time, seize the obnoxious arachnid with forceps and gently, but steadily, pull it off your lizard. Save the tick for later identification by preserving it in alcohol. Apply some topical antibiotic to the area where you extracted the tick. Do not buy a specimen that is infested with ticks, but if by some misfortune you have an infested animal you can safely treat it with a spray or powder form of some "tickacide" containing pyrethrins or carbaryl (Sevin). Just be sure to avoid the eyes, ears, mouth, and vent area.

Mites: Monitors are not good candidates for harboring mites, the bane of snake keepers, but they may sometimes be seen on imported animals or they may get to your lizards if you introduce an infested reptile to your collection without implementing proper quarantine procedures. Infested animals will show signs of irritation and may be seen to be rubbing up against the sides of the enclosure or soaking themselves more often than usual. Sometimes these parasites specifically attack the eyes and if not treated, can cause severe eye infections (from excessive rubbing against objects). While pyrethrins or Sevin can be used to treat most infestations (except eye infestations), Vapona No Pest Strips® (2.2 dichlorovinyl dimethyl phosphate) usually will take care of the problem very well. Use a small section of strip (about 1 or 2 in.) wrapped in a small piece of nylon screen and suspend it in the cage by attaching this to a length of thin wire (such as a "twist-tie" used for closing plastic bags). Remove all water, food, cage furniture, and substrate, and leave the strip for 2 to 4 days. It may help to place a small piece of this strip in a plastic trash bag together with any cage furniture or empty water bowls. Clean and disinfect the cage. Repeat the procedure for the same length of time about 3 weeks later. Disinfect all cage furniture before putting it back.

There is one disadvantage to Vapona® treatment. Some lizards seem to be particularly prone to idiosyncratic responses to this chemical. In other words, it could prove toxic to your pet. Symptoms of a toxic reaction will often include a chronic, progressive, total paralysis of the lizard that seems to **always** be fatal! Prolonged or high dose exposure to these pest strips can also cause liver damage. This author once lost a beautiful Dumeril's monitor to this treatment. However, this remedy is one of the most effective at eliminating mites, and most monitors so treated by the author have had no ill effects.

Internal parasites
The main internal parasites found to be potential problems for monitors are tapeworms, some digestive tract inhabiting nematodes, and a few protozoans, like *Entamoeba invadens* or some coccidia. Always quarantine all new lizards and have fecal samples checked by a qualified veterinarian to identify internal parasites and prescribe the best course of treatment. This author always quarantines new animals and ensures that neither they nor anything from their cages ever contacts other specimens until they have been found parasite-free (internal and external).

NUTRITIONAL DISORDERS
If your savannah monitor is getting the proper diet, these problems should not appear in your animal. However, it may be appropriate to list a few potential troublemakers.

a. **Metabolic bone disease/calcium deficiency.** This will normally not be a problem with adult savannah monitors, but it could become one if one is not careful when feeding monitor babies. Calcium deficiency is not simply a lack of available calcium, because simply adding supplemental calcium will not solve the problem. The proper absorption of calcium, via the intestinal lining is accomplished with an adequate amount of vitamin D3 and a proper calcium/phosphorus ratio. Lizards seem to require 1 to 2 parts calcium to 1 part phosphorus. The reason why babies can be a source of trouble is because some beginning herpetoculturists may exclusively feed them crickets and/or "pinky" mice. These are not totally balanced diets and should be supplemented with a mineral/vitamin mix. For those who use insects to feed very young monitors, this author recommends consulting Philippe de Vosjoli's "The Right Way to Feed Insect-eating Lizards", which is another book in the Herpetological Library series. One method to properly ensure good nutrition in baby monitors is to get them to occasionally (about 1-2 times per month) eat canned cat (preferred by this author) or dog food. Use poultry flavors which are more "natural" and somewhat less fatty. One of the major brands (such as Purina ® or Alpo ®) will be sufficient. By doing this, the author has never encountered metabolic bone disease in monitors.

The symptoms of calcium deficiencies in lizards are usually "soft" jaws and/or back and limb deformities (in juveniles), and swollen "smooth" hind limbs, and/

or swollen deformed lower jaws in adults. The latter symptoms are indicative of a condition whereby the animal compensates for thin and weak bones by depositing spongy tissue. In monitors, this should **NEVER** be allowed to become a problem!

b. **Induced thiamine (vitamin B1) deficiency.** This can be a problem for some monitor lizards, particularly Nile monitors or water monitors fed almost exclusively on thawed, frozen fish. If the fish is oily, steatitis (inflammation of fat, which will require vitamin E treatment) can also be a problem. The most common symptom is twitching of limbs or fine muscular tremors. Muscular atrophy can result if this condition is left untreated too long. Change the diet, and if symptoms are severe, consult a veterinarian. This should not normally be a problem with savannah monitors because fish is not recommended as a dietary staple.

c. **Induced biotin deficiency.** This is a problem seen in monitor lizards that are fed largely on raw non-embryonated whole eggs. This is because raw egg white contains avidin which induces this deficiency. Change the diet to a more varied and balanced diet and avoid raw eggs because of the additional hazard of Salmonellosis.

d. **Obesity.** If your adult monitor is overfed and inactive, it **will** become very fat. If this is allowed to continue, the fat may be deposited in the internal organs, especially the liver, with potentially fatal results. Curtail overfeeding and restrict your animal's intake if it is becoming too fat. Encourage it to exercise by providing it with adequate space to move about and explore. Monitor lizards are very active in the wild and appear to patrol fairly large territories in search of food.

RESPIRATORY INFECTIONS

Respiratory infections usually result from keeping savannah monitors (and other species) at temperatures that are not warm enough. This results in lowering the lizards resistance to infections and creates a situation where the immune system cannot function properly. Elevated mucus content is usually noted in the mouth and nostrils, and the mucus may appear somewhat foamy. In young animals, gently pressing the thumb against the throat will cause mucus to exude from the nostrils. Other early symptoms are: sluggishness, decreased or lack of appetite and slightly labored breathing. Slight gaping and puffing of air in and out of the throat and lungs are sure indications of pneumonia. The sick lizard will spend much of its time with its eyes closed. As the disease progresses, all these symptoms will worsen and the animal will begin to spend time with its head elevated and bubbly mucus will begin to exude from the mouth and nose. If the disease is discovered early, elevated temperatures in the upper 80's to lower 90's °F (30-32°C) will help the monitor fight off the infection. If it does not improve after a few days of elevated temperature, then treatment with injectable antibiotics will be required. A veterinarian should be consulted as early as possible to determine and administer the most effective antibiotics. Drinking water must be available at all times during the course of treatment.

GASTROINTESTINAL DISEASES

Occasionally, savannah monitors may develop diarrhea, which may be discolored, foul smelling, and/or bloody. This condition can occur in imported animals and in established animals that are fed raw chicken parts or rotten prey or kept with foul water on a regular basis. Inadequate maintenance temperatures also contribute to the susceptibility to pathogens. If the symptoms persist for more than a few days, your monitor may have a serious gastroenteric disease. Consult a veterinarian for diagnosis and treatment. Do not allow this to go untreated for long! With early diagnosis and treatment, the prognosis for recovery is usually good.

EYE DISEASES

According to Dr. Frederic Frye (1981, 1991), monitor lizards may be prone to juvenile cataracts, which occurs most often in young lizards. It is not clear why this should occur, but Dr. Frye suspects it could possibly be dietary. Whatever the cause, Dr. Frye thinks this reflects an "idiosyncrasy of monitor lizards" (1981, p.237). The cataracts can vary in their severity. Some monitors appear to suffer little from this condition, while others show virtual blindness, especially in low light. There is no treatment. The author has, so far, not observed this syndrome in any savannah monitors.

A hatchling Dumeril's monitor (*Varanus dumerilii*). Photo by Glen Carlzen.

Breeding

To date there has been no consistent, repeated captive breeding of any monitor species with the exception of the Australian spiny-tailed monitor *Varanus acanthurus*. The fact is that there is no formula for the breeding of monitor lizards as there is for the breeding of many other reptiles. The small number of breeding records and the generally poor breeding success can in part be attributed to minimal efforts by members of the private sector to develop the commercial breeding of monitor lizards. At this point in time, the space, costs and labor of developing captive breeding of monitor lizards does not appear to be a profitable venture particularly with the less expensive species now imported in large numbers. Possibly better management of wild populations and the development of field culture in the countries of origin are a better course of action with the larger species. Nonetheless, more efforts should be made in this area by hobbyists, particularly with the rarer species, to develop a methodology for sustained multigeneration propagation. The knowledge derived from developing this methodology may prove invaluable in the future conservation of varanid species. If you are keeping one monitor lizard, why don't you consider obtaining a mate for it?

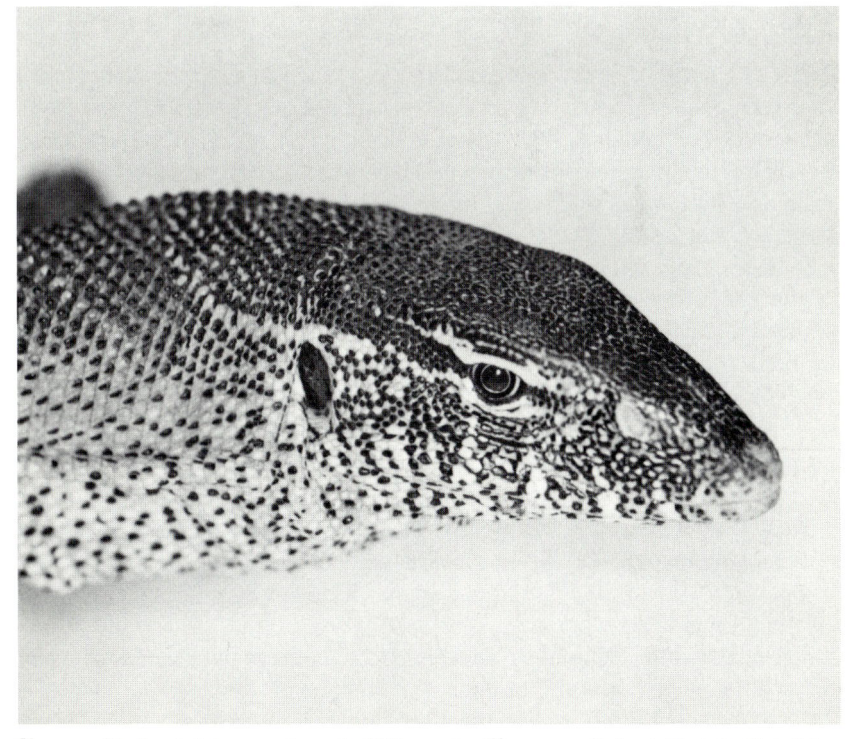

Close-up of the head of a tame captive-raised Nile monitor (*Varanus n. niloticus*). Photo by Chris Estep.

For those wishing to attempt to breed monitor lizards, the following are guidelines which could contribute to success (remember there is no established breeding formula).

1) If possible, start with captive-raised animals. There are indications that captive-raised monitors may breed more readily than imported adults.

2) Try to determine the sex of your animals. Without at least one sexual pair you have no chance of breeding your animals. If you have the facilities to maintain several pairs, your chances of success will be greatly increased. There will be a greater probability that some pairs will breed some of the time. If one pair does not seem interested, try switching partners.

3) Your savannah monitors should be sexually mature. They should be at least two and a half years (under optimal conditions) and preferably three years or more if captive-raised. The growth rate of adult monitors is drastically reduced compared to that of immature monitors and reduced growth rate can possibly be used as a criterion for sexual maturity. Finally, size is a valid criterion. Savannah monitors three feet or greater in length are virtually certain to be sexually mature animals.

4) The animals should have good weight but should not be grossly obese.

5) Create a period of rest/cooling/fasting. As a rule, many reptiles do not breed when environmental conditions remain constant and this appears to be true with many species of monitors. With savannah monitors, a rest period can be induced in early fall though some private breeders have successfully induced breeding in white-throated monitors (*Varanus exanthematicus albigularis*) by cooling them in the winter. Remember, this subspecies of the savannah monitor comes from areas of Southern Africa that has a cool period where the temperature significantly drops for an extended period of time. One successful zoo breeding of the latter subspecies occurred following a very brief winter cooling. A period of rest/inactivity usually induced through a period of cooling and fasting that may also include a period of reduced day length, will often alter physiological pathways in reptiles resulting in subsequent reproductive processes and behaviors. A methodology for inducing a rest period in savannah monitors should include:

a) Keep pairs separate.
b) Reduce the temperature range at which the animals are maintained by 10 °F (mid to upper 60's to lower 70's at night and upper 70's to low 80's during the day) for a period of four to six weeks.
c) During that time, reduce the photoperiod to 10 hours of light versus 14 hours of darkness. This should also result in 14 hours of night cooling.
d) Have the animals fast, or feed them very reduced amounts.

6) After the rest period, re-establish temperatures, preferably in the high range and raise the photoperiod to 14 or more hours of daylight per day (up to 24 hours has been recommended by some herpetoculturists to induce breeding), feed heavily and supplement the diet with a vitamin/mineral supplement. During the following weeks, introduce the female into the male's vivarium for one to three days at a time at regular intervals (every week to ten days). Keep animals under surveillance, because some animals may fight. Do not confuse combat with mating behavior.

7) Once copulatory attempts cease, the animals should be kept separated. If successful breeding has occurred, egg-laying will usually follow four to six weeks after the observation of copulation.

8) The eggs (about 3.7 cm to 4.5 cm) can be incubated in moist sand or moistened vermiculite (50% vermiculite and 50% water by weight) at 85-86F (29-30°C). They should hatch in 116-180 days.

The above is a hypothetical model which will have to be confirmed and very likely, drastically modified through experimentation. Possibly only a very brief rest period is required. Possibly environmental changes other than a cool rest period will be the key triggers to successful breeding. There's lots of room for original and worthwhile research in this area and you don't have to be a Ph.D to accomplish good work as long as you keep careful and meticulous records.

For more information on the breeding of monitor lizards, the following will be very useful references:

1. Auffenberg, Walter. 1983. Courtship behavior in *Varanus bengalensis* (Sauria: Varanidae). In: A.G.J. Rhodinl and K.Miyata (eds.). Advances in Herpetology and Evolutionary Biology:Essays in Honor of Ernest E. Williams. Cambridge:Mus. Comp. Zool., Harvard University. pp. 535-51.

2. David, Reuben. 1970. Breeding the mugger crocodile and water monitor *Crocodylus palustris* and *Varanus salvator* at the Ahmedabad Zoo. Int. Zoo Yb. 10: pp. 116-117.

3. Horn, Hans-Georg & Gerard J. Visser. 1989. Review of reproduction of monitor lizards *Varanus spp.* in captivity. Int. Zoo Yb. 28: pp. 140-150.

4. Radford, Larry & Frederick L. Paine. 1989. The reproduction and management of the Dumeril's monitor. Int. Zoo Yb. 28: pp. 153-155.

5. Sprackland, Robert G. 1991. Mating and waiting: A status report on reproduction in captive monitor lizards (Sauria: Varanidae). In: Gowen, Ralph L. (ed.) Captive Propagation and Husbandry of Reptiles and Amphibians 1989. Northern California Herpetological Society, Special Publication #5. pp. 57-63.

6. Visser, G.J. 1981. Breeding the white-throated monitor *Varanus exanthematicus albigularis* at the Rotterdam Zoo. Int. Zoo Yb. 21: pp. 87-91.

Adult Timor monitor (*Varanus timorensis*). Because of their small size, dwarf monitors are generally better candidates for breeding projects. Photo by Glen Carlzen.

"Goliath", a tame savannah monitor resting on top of its cage in an apartment in New York City. Photo by Philippe de Vosjoli.

Immature Dumeril's or brown rough-necked monitor. Overall, this is a docile and easily maintained species. It has recently been successfully bred in captivity. Photo by Glen Carlzen.

Mangrove monitor (*Varanus indicus*) performing an aggressive display. These animals are currently being imported in small numbers from the Solomon Islands. Photo by Glen Carlzen.

Notes On Other Monitor Species

The Dumeril's Monitor. (*Varanus dumerilii*)

The Dumeril's monitor is a modest sized Southeast Asian species which includes two generally similar appearing subspecies (*V. d. heterophilis* and *V. d. dumerilii*). This species attains average adult lengths of about 4 feet (1.2 m) and occurs in the Malay Peninsula and parts of Indochina. In the pet trade, it is often referred to as the brown rough-necked monitor. As babies, Dumeril's monitors are very strikingly colored with beautiful yellow to almost orangish heads and gorgeous alternating broad yellow and black stripes. As adults, this pattern dulls considerably. This species is well known for its ability to tame easily (many become "dog tame") and adapts very well as a captive. Dumeril's monitor is partially arboreal and has a highly keeled tail for swimming and climbing. This is a rainforest species and thus needs a rather humid and warm climate, about 85-95°F (29-35°C) during the day and about 75°F (24°C) at night. To properly maintain this species you should provide thick branches or large cork sections to climb upon. This species loves to soak so provide an extra large water container (such as a large cat litter box) or some sort of self-draining pool setup. In the author's opinion, this species makes one of the best captive monitors, perhaps even better than the savannah monitor, if you can provide the proper conditions. Dumeril's monitor is now becoming difficult to obtain and is rather expensive when available.

The Mangrove Monitor. (*Varanus indicus*)

This is a species consisting of three somewhat similar appearing subspecies (*V.i. spinulosus*, *V.i. indicus*, and *V.i. kalabeck*) that is distributed throughout Australasia, particularly northwestern Australia, New Guinea, the Indo-Malayan archipelago, and some of the islands in the western Pacific, including the Solomon Islands. It inhabits estuarine mangrove areas, monsoon vine forests, semi-open areas, and thick forests. Mangrove monitors are often seen basking on branches overhanging water and will hide inside hollow limbs and tree trunks. This is another moderate sized monitor, reaching a length of as much as 4.9 ft (1.5 m) though most imports seldom exceed 3.5 ft. This animal has beautiful colors with the top and sides being a dark olive to blackish-green, speckled with small yellow to yellow-orange spots. The belly is largely whitish or whitish-yellow with very small blackish spots, almost the reverse of the dorsal pattern.

The mangrove monitor is highly carnivorous and, in the wild, feeds on virtually any vertebrate prey it can catch as well as invertebrates including crabs. The juveniles will devour insects. The author is particularly fond of this species, despite its somewhat "skittish" behavior as a captive, but perhaps this is because

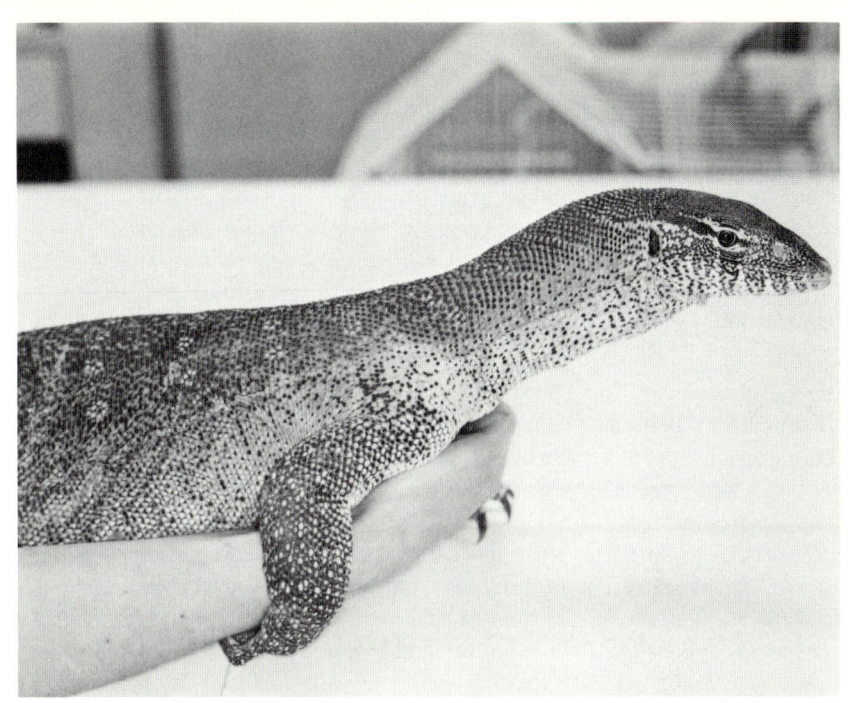

A three year old captive-raised and tame adult Nile monitor. This is *Varanus niloticus niloticus*.

A tame adult Burundi or ornate Nile monitor *(Varanus niloticus ornatus)*. Photo by Greg Naclerio.

all the specimens obtained are wild-caught adults. Mangrove monitors have voracious appetites and will readily accept adult mice. They spend a lot of time hiding in the substrate and do not seem to move about much. They do love to climb, and they should be provided with branches to climb upon. They also frequent water and enjoy long soaks (like most monitors they will defecate in the water). They should be maintained like Dumeril's monitor. They have very powerful claws and rather large teeth, so care should be given when handling. This species is also infamous for defecating when handled as a defense mechanism (so keep that vent away from your clothing). In addition, mangrove monitors move remarkably fast and are notorious escape artists! Most imported specimens are from the Solomon Islands.

The Nile Monitor. *(Varanus niloticus)*

This is the largest lizard (up to 7 feet or 2.1 m) found in Africa. Nile monitors are found throughout sub-Saharan Africa, along the Nile River into Egypt, as well as over much of the rest of Africa along rivers and other aquatic habitats, along sandy and tree-covered banks. Most specimens for the pet trade are imported from Kenya, Nigeria, and Togo. They show striking and somewhat variable color patterns (depending on the area of origin) and are classified as two major subspecies by Mertens, *V. n. niloticus*, and *V. n. ornatus*. This monitor is semi-aquatic (has a highly keeled tail), but spends the early part of its day sunning itself on rocky outcrops, tree stumps, and sandy or muddy islets. It is an active, voracious predator on crabs, mollusks, frogs, fish, reptiles, birds, and small mammals and is a major and notorious predator upon Nile crocodile eggs. These animals will flee when threatened (read: handled) and will probably lash with their tails and attempt to bite when cornered (read: picked up).

These can be among the most wary and aggressive monitors and many do not tame (especially wild-caught adults). This author does not recommend this species unless one is willing to spend plenty of time taming it. The initial selection of your Nile monitor will be critical (preferably hatchlings or young animals) and frequent handling of an initially tame specimen is essential. Nile monitors are one of the most commonly available monitors, second only to the savannah monitor. They generally fare well in captivity. These lizards are **very** powerful and require great respect.

They are fairly rough in texture, and the adults range from greyish-brown to dark olive brown up top of the head and back. This basic color is mottled with scattered dark blotches and pale yellow spots and/or bands on the head, back, and limbs. The belly and throat are pale with some blackbars. Juveniles are beautifully colored with black and yellow. It is common for pet stores to confuse this species with the more desirable Asian water monitor (*V. salvator*). The easiest way to distinguish the two is to note the position of the nostrils. Nile monitors have their nostrils located high, but somewhat laterally on their snouts, while water monitors have

Timor monitor (*Varanus timorensis similis*). These monitors are currently being imported in small numbers from Indonesia. Their small size makes them ideal for keeping in attractive, naturalistic displays and for captive breeding. Photo by Glen Carlzen.

Black tree monitors (*Varanus prasinus beccarii*). It has recently been suggested that this subspecies of tree monitor should be raised to full species status. Their general care is similar to that of green tree monitors. Black tree monitors have recently been bred in captivity. Photo by Glen Carlzen.

Green tree monitor *(Varanus prasinus)*. This species feeds primarily on insects and other arthropods. In captivity their diet is also supplemented with occasional feedings of pink or early stage fuzzy mice. All imports should be checked and treated for internal parasites. Flagellate protozoans are common in imports. Photo by Glen Carlzen.

Black rough-neck monitor *(Varanus rudicollis)*. The large raised scales on the neck and the long, thin bird-like head are characteristics of this interesting species. All imported specimens should be checked by a veterinarian for internal parasites and treated accordingly. Photo by Chris Estep.

them much closer to the tip of the snout, and more toward the top than sides. Nile monitors can be kept like savannah monitors, except that this species will require a large water container for soaking. A filtered or easily drained pool is highly desirable when keeping this species.

The Tree Monitor. *(Varanus prasinus)*
The tree monitor *(Varanus prasinus)* consists of three subspecies: *V. p. prasinus* which is often referred to as the green tree monitor and usually shows narrow black crossbanding, *V. p. kordensis* which is also green with a black net-like pattern, and *V. p. beccarii* (Sprackland (1991b) calls this a separate species. *V. beccarii)* which is all black. The black subspecies is also found in Australia on the eastern Cape York peninsula and Torres Strait Islands (Queensland), but all three races are found in New Guinea or its associated islands. Australian specimens are found in or near vine forests, particularly those found near water, and are found at altitudes of 197-1772 ft (60-540 m) in Australia's McIlwraith Range. This lizard also likes monsoon, palm, rain, and mangrove forests. They are highly arboreal and dwell mostly high up in the canopy. They have a prehensile tail, and somewhat sticky, soft, black-colored tissue on the soles of their feet. They have pale yellow-green bellies. These monitors are relatively small, averaging a total length of 1.5-2.5 ft (0.5-0.75 m). Tree monitors seem to feed almost exclusively upon insects and other terrestrial arthropods. They also take small lizards (such as geckos and skinks) and small birds and their eggs. They **require** a setup that allows them ample area to climb, which means providing them with branches or small trees. They will need temperatures and humidity like the Dumeril's monitor.

The Black Rough-Necked Monitor. *(Varanus rudicollis)*
This is a very interesting and rather bizarre looking monitor from the Malay Peninsula, Borneo, and other islands in the immediate vicinity. Black rough-necked monitors reach an average length of about 4 ft (1.2 m) and tend to be arboreal. Wild-caught adults often do not thrive, but very young specimens do reasonably well. As a whole, this is not a very aggressive species. Adults are largely dark black with a few yellow cross bands and have very narrow, long, almost bird-like heads. They feed upon terrestrial arthropods and microhylid frogs in the wild, but will readily feed on rodents, eggs and baby chickens as captives. This species requires a setup similar to the Dumeril's monitor and enjoys something to climb upon. All imported specimens should be checked for flagellate protozoans. Sometimes the difference between establishing in captivity and death is simply a treatment with Flagyl (metronidazole). Some herpetoculturists suspect that this species may be social. Sometimes, keeping two animals together may be beneficial.

An immature crocodile monitor *(Varanus salvadorii)*. Juveniles and immature animals have bright yellow and sometimes bluish speckling which will fade as animals become older. This species can only be recommended to individuals willing to provide the room-sized enclosures that these animals will eventually require. Photo by Glen Carlzen.

An adult crocodile monitor *(Varanus salvadorii)*. Photo by Glen Carlzen.

The Crocodile Montior. *(Varanus salvadorii)*
This monitor also goes under the name of Papuan monitor and obviously, hails from the jungles of New Guinea. It is a very large species that can reach total lengths of 9 or more feet (3m+) and rivals the Komodo monitor (*Varanus komodoensis*) for size, though the latter is much more robust and heavier in build. This lizard is olive-brown to dark blackish-brown with yellow spots. "Crocodile" monitor seems almost a misnomer, considering that this lizard is largely arboreal. It feeds almost exclusively upon birds and their eggs, and like emerald tree boas, have very long sharp teeth adapted for this purpose. It has a very distinctive head which ends in a peculiarly bulbous nose. It is apparently uncommon and commands very high prices ($1000 or more). It requires a room-sized enclosure designed like the setup for Dumeril's monitors. Large branches should be provided for climbing. This species is not a good choice, unless you can provide it with the large amount of space it requires. They have incredibly long tails which they may use as weapons and can inflict deep, nasty bites that usually require stitches.

The Water Monitor. *(Varanus salvator)*
This species is very popular and is also often called the Asian water monitor. It is similar in appearance to the Nile monitor (see section about Nile monitor), so be careful to be able to distinguish the two species. This species consists of six subspecies: *V. s. salvator*, *V. s. togianus*, *V. s. marmoratus*, *V. s. cumingi*, *V. s. nuchalis*, and *V. s. scutigerulus*. It is perhaps, the most ubiquitous monitor lizard in Asia, and ranges from Sri Lanka, India, Indochina, south China, northern Australia (presumably), the Malay Peninsula and the various islands of Malaysia, the Philippines, New Guinea, and other islands in the Indian Ocean and South China Sea. As babies, these lizards are black above, with large and small yellow spots arranged in a transverse series. There are yellow and black bars along the sides of the snout and lips and a fairly wide black transverse bar runs across the eye to behind the ear. The limbs have yellow-white spots on black. The belly is yellow with narrow, often V-shaped black bands. As these lizards mature the markings become less distinct with adults often appearing dark blackish-olive above with indistinct yellow or white spots.

Water monitors grow to rather large sizes, achieving total lengths of 6-7 feet (about 2+ meters) on average. Their tails are as long or slightly longer than their bodies ($SVL = 1$ m, tail length $= 1$ m to 1.5 m). This species is highly aquatic and will appreciate a container to soak in and/or swim. Water monitors can be kept in setups like that for Dumeril's monitors, but must be provided with larger enclosures, at least 6+ feet long and 4+ feet wide. This species will climb to some degree, though not like crocodile monitors, Dumeril's monitors, or black rough-neck monitors. They will eat all sorts of vertebrates, large insects, crustaceans, and some mollusks, and in the wild will feast on crocodile and turtle eggs and even turtles. In captivity they fare well on rodents. If acquired as small specimens, they can usually be readily tamed, and "dog tame" large water monitors are not uncommon. For readers who have seen the recent motion picture, "The Freshman", the lizard masquerading as a Komodo dragon was actually a water monitor. These lizards are not as easy to obtain as they were 7-10 years ago and are significantly more expensive than they were then.

A young water monitor (*Varanus salvator*). Juveniles of this species are quite calm compared to juvenile Nile monitors. As with all imported Asian monitors, treatment of internal parasites is essential for establishing these animals in captivity. Photo by Glen Carlzen.

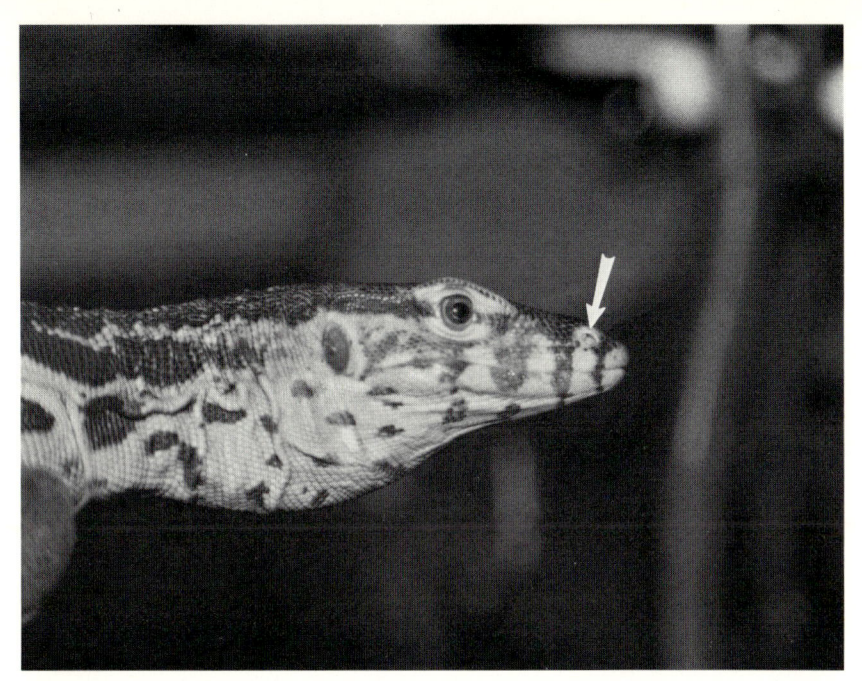

An immature water monitor *(Varanus salvator)*. Note the anterior position of the nostril compared to a Nile monitor's. Photo by Ned Gilmore.

A subadult Nile monitor *(Varanus niloticus)*. Note the position of the nostril compared to a Malayan water monitor. Also note the thick leather gloves used in handling. Photo by Edward Gilmore.

Source Materials

What follows is a list of sources that were not mentioned earlier in the text.

Aufenberg, Walter. 1978. Social and feeding behavior in *Varanus komodoensis*. In: Neil Greenberg and Paul D. MacLean (eds.). Behavior and Neurology of Lizards An Interdisciplinary Colloquium. National Institute of Mental Halth, Rockville, MD. pp. 301-331.

Auffenberg, Walter. 1981. The Behavioral Ecology of the Komodo Monitor. University of Florida Press, Gainesville, FL. p. 406.

Auffenberg, Walter. 1988. Gray's Monitor Lizard. University of Florida Press, Gainesville, FL. p. 419.

Balsai, Michael J. 1990. Monitors: Dragons in captivity. Reptile & Ampibian Magazine. July-August 1990: pp. 2-5 & pp. 46-48.

Balsai, Michael J. 1991. Two wide ranging "Asian" Monitors. VaraNews 1(6): pp. 5-7.

Bayless, Mark K. 1991. A trip to Africa. VaraNews 1(5): pp. 5-8.

Branch, Bill. 1988. Field Guide to the Snakes and other Reptiles of Southern Africa. Ralph Curtis, Sanibel Island, FL. p. 326.

Bohme, W. et. al. 1989. A new monitor lizard (Reptilia: Varanidae) from Yemen, with notes on ecology, phylogeny, and zoogeography. In: Buttiker, W. & F. Krupp (eds.). Fauna of Saudi Arabia. Vol. 10. pp. 433-448.

Cogger, Harold G. 1986. Reptiles and Amphibians of Australia. Reed Books Pty. Ltd. NSW, Australia. p. 688.

Funk, Richard S. and Philip R. Vilaro. 1980. An English translation of Robert Mertens' Keys to the monitor lizards, with a list of currently recognized species and subspecies. Bulletin of the Chicago Herpetological Society 15(2): pp. 31-46.

Greer, Allen E. 1989. The Biology & Evolution of Australian Lizards. Surrey Beatty & Sons Pty Limited, NSW, Australia. p. 264.

Holmes, Roger S. et al. 1975. Phenetic relationships among varanid lizards based upon comparative electrophoretic data and karyotypic analysis. Biochem. System. Ecol. 3: pp. 257-262.

Inskipp, Tim. 1982. World trade in monitor lizard skins, 1977 - 1982. Traffic Bulletin VI(3/4): pp. 51-53.

Inskipp, Tim. 1981. Indian Trade in Reptile Skin. Conservation Monitoring Centre, Cambridge, UK. p. 13.

King, Dennis & Brian Green. 1979. Notes on diet and reproduction of the sand goanna *Varanus gouldii rosenbergii*. Copea 1979(1): pp. 64-70.

King, Max and Dennis King. 1975. Chromosomal evolution in the lizard genus *Varanus* (Reptilia). Aust. J. Biol. Sci. 28: pp. 89-1O8.

King, Max. 1990. Chromosomal and immunogenetic data: A new perspective on the origin of Australia's reptiles. In: Olmo, Ettore (ed.) Cytogenetics of Amphibians and Reptiles. Birkhauser Verlag, Basel, Switzerland. pp. 153-180.

Laurent, R.F. 1964. A new subspecies of *Varanus exanthematicus* (Sauria, Varanidae). Breviora (199): pp. 1-9.

Losos, Jonathan B. & Harry W. Greene. 1988. Ecological and evolutionary implications of diet in monitor lizards. Biological Journal of the Linnean Society 35: pp. 379-407.

Luxmoore, Richard & B. Groombridge. 1989. Asian Monitor Lizards: A Review of Distribution, Status, Exploitation and Trade in Four Selected Species. (Draft Report to CITES Secretariat). World Conservation Monitoring Centre. Cambridge, UK. p. 190.

Luxmoore, Richard, et al. (eds.). 1988. Significant Trade in Wildlife: A Review of Selected Species in CITE'S Appendix II. Volume 2: Reptiles and Invertebrates. International Union for Conservation of Nature and Natural Resources. Cambridge, UK. p. 306.

Mertens, Robert. 1942. Die Familie der Warane (*Varanidae*). Abhandlungen der Senckenbergischen Naturforschenden Gesellschaft, 462: pp. 1-116; 465: pp. 117-234; 466: pp. 235-391.

McCoy, Michael. 1980. Reptiles of the Solomon Islands: Wau Institute Handbook # 7. Wau, Papua, New Guinea. p. 80.

Ross, Richard A. & Gerald Marzec. 1990. The Reproductive Husbandry of Pythons and Boas. Institute for Herpetological Research. Stanford, CA. p. 270.

Shea, Glenn M. and Gary L. Reddacliff. 1986. Ossifications in the hemipenes of varanids. J. Herpetology 20(4): pp. 566-568.

Smith, Malcolm A. 1935. (Repr. 1973). The Fauna of British India: Reptilia and Amphibia, Vol. 2: Sauria. Ralph Curtis Books, Hollywood, FL. p.440. (This is the reprint publisher).

Sprackland, Robert G. 1990. A preliminary study of food discrimination in monitor lizards (Reptilia: Lacertilia: Varanidae). Bulletin of the Chicago Herpetological Society 25(10): pp. 181-183.

Sprackland, Robert G. 199la. A myriad of monitors. Tropical Fish Hobbyist. January 1991: pp. 130-138.

Sprackland, Robert G. 199lb. The emerald tree monitor, *Varanus prasinus*. Tropical Fish Hobbyist. January 1991: pp. 110-114.

Storr, G.M., L.A. Smith, & R.E. Johnstone. 1983. Lizards of Western Australia, Vol.2: Dragons and Monitors. Western Australian Museum, Belmont, Western Australia. p. 113.

Stewart, James S. 1989. Techniques for sex identification in large reptiles. In: Gowen, Ralph L. (ed.) Captive Propagation and Husbandry of Captive Reptiles and Amphibians. Northern California Herpetological Society, Special Publication #5. pp. 57-63

Strimple, Pete. 1988. The savannah monitor, *Varanus exanthematicus* (Bosc, 1792). Part 1. The Forked Tongue 13(12): pp. 8-13.

Strimple, Pete. 1989. The savannah monitor, *Varanus exanthematicus* (Bosc, 1792). Part 2. The Forked Tongue 14(1): pp. 5-7.

Strimple, Pete. 1989. The savannah monitor, *Varanus exanthematicus* (Bosc, 1792). Part 3. The Forked Tongue 14(2): pp. 5-8.

Strimple, Pete. 1989. The savannah monitor, *Varanus exanthematicus* (Bosc, 1792). Part 4. The Forked Tongue 14(3): pp. 7-16.

Strimple, Pete. 1989. Observations on three captive juvenile West African savanna monitors, *Varanus e. exanthematicus* (Bosc, 1792). Notes to NOAH XVI(10): 8-12. (Reprinted in VaraNews. 1990. 1(2): pp.6-8).

Taylor, Edward H. 1963. The lizards of Thailand. University of Kansas Science Bulletin LXIV: pp. 687-1077.

Weigel, John. 1988. Care of Australian Reptiles in Captivity. Reptile Keepers Association, Gosford, NSW, Australia. p. 144.

Wilson, Stephen K. & David G. Knowles. 1988. Australia's Reptiles: A photographic Reference to the Terrestrial Reptiles of Australia. Collins, Sydney, NSW, Australia. pp. 447.

Wynne, Richard H. 1981. Lizards in Captivity. TFH Publications, Neptune City, N.J. p. 189.

Zimmerman, Elke. 1986. Breeding Terrarium Animals. TFH Publications, Neptune City, N.J. p. 384.

Looking for more information? Varanix, the Varanid Information eXchange offers its members a bi-monthly newsletter dedicated to the responsible care of varanids in captivity through education and the open exchange of information.

Membership:
One-year membership in Varanix is:
-$10 US/year (USA)
-$12 US/year (foreign)

Address all inquiries and memberships to:
Greg Naclerio
Varanix
8726D S.Sepulveda Bl. #243
Los Angeles, CA 90045 USA
Ph: (310) 768-8669